DI022427

From
Father to Father

LETTERS FROM LOSS DAD TO LOSS DAD

From Father to Father © 2016 Emily R. Long

Printed in the United States of America
First Printing 2016
ISBN: 978-0-9965556-4-7

Firefly Grace Publishing
Burlington, VT 05403
www.EmilyRLong.com

Interior and Cover Design: ShiftFWD
Cover Photo: Todd Quackenbush

In memory of Ryan
Honoring the father you never got to be to the daughter you
never got to know.
You would have been an amazing dad.

For all the fathers of loss,
too often unseen and unacknowledged.
We honor you and your amazing father love.

DEAR FATHERS,

Th is book is for you. It is written by fathers of loss for fathers of loss. It has been my honor to collect these letters from fathers from around the world. These fathers came together to contribute to this book and offer their words, their support, and their understanding to other fathers like you – fathers grieving and missing their precious children.

It has been apparent to me the lack of resources and support specifically for fathers of loss. Too often it seems that all the focus, attention, and care is directed toward mothers of loss and that fathers can be forgotten and disregarded.

You are not forgotten. A father's love is an irreplaceable gift and your children have been blessed with this gift. You deserve all the support, care, and love in the world as you learn to live with this loss.

My hope is that this book can offer some of that support and care and love – even if only in a small way. I hope that it can help bring fathers together to lean on each other and to support each other in a way that feels nurturing and beneficial and comforting.

Most of all, I want you to know that you are not alone. If you feel forgotten, if you feel lost, if you feel alone – I hope that this book will bring you a sense of acknowledgement, recognition, and not-alone-ness.

You are an amazing father. Your children are so very lucky to have you as their dad.

xoxo,
Emily

LETTERS

TO OTHER FATHERS OF LOSS,

I have been where you are. Each stage of the grief so different yet so familiar. I recommend leaving your pride at the door to really open up and feel your feelings. Do not be too proud to crumble under the weight of your grief. Do not try and be everything to everyone else and leave nothing for you. The emptiness left over will do nothing for your healing, but will allow that emptiness to be filled with anger, resentment, aggression, rage, sorrow, depression, and other emotions that prevent you from healing.

Grab your emotions from the sky like a lightning bolt and embrace the electric ride, a ride you will be on for the rest of your life. When you reach for that lightning bolt, you had better be prepared to know how you will control the power of those emotions. Will you hold on too tight and squeeze until nothing else can be allowed in? Will you be consumed by the pure emotions of the loss of your child(ren)? Or will you grab it carefully and be able to live life while feeling your emotions? Will you simply not reach for that lightning bolt at all because it will hurt too much? Or is it a combination of every option?

At times through my grief I have done all of the above. I have grabbed on so tight all I felt was pain and sorrow, then I had to lessen my grip and I was able to love others again the way they deserved. At times I have not reached for that bolt of lightning and denied my emotions so I could live in the moment without the storm clouds of grief above me.

We must be able to find the right grip on our grief to be who we need to be in our lives. Whatever your family constellation is and your role in that as a father and man you need to figure that grip out. Will your grip change from time to time and situation to situation? Yes. What we must figure out is the range of control over our grief that will allow us to be the best fathers and the best men we can. At the 2016 American School Counselors Association annual conference, keynote speaker Lt. Gen. Russel L. Honore stated that "*We must save our best leadership for when we get home, for our family time*". I take these words seriously and have tried to live by them since I have heard them. These words mean to not only show emotions while you are home but to be true to your emotions. If you are having a bad day, do not try and be everything to everyone and leave nothing for yourself. Model your emotions and feel your emotions. Release the social stigma that men do not show emotions - your child(ren) have died and emotions will feel like a lightning strike, often fast, fierce, out of nowhere, and intense.

Fathers of loss, we must show our emotions and not be afraid or ashamed in doing so. We are human and showing our emotions is an opportunity to heal and learn. Showing our emotions in difficult times does not make us weak or not powerful. In reality it does the exact opposite. We show we are human, we have emotions, and that we love our child who died so deeply that we show emotions while controlling the lightning.

William Skaggs III

Father to Michael Joseph "MJ" Skaggs
https://www.facebook.com/mjsmemories/

"FATHERS OF LOSS, WE MUST SHOW OUR EMOTIONS AND NOT BE AFRAID OR ASHAMED IN DOING SO. WE ARE HUMAN AND SHOWING OUR EMOTIONS IS AN OPPORTUNITY TO HEAL AND LEARN. SHOWING OUR EMOTIONS IN DIFFICULT TIMES DOES NOT MAKE US WEAK OR NOT POWERFUL. IN REALITY IT DOES THE EXACT OPPOSITE. WE SHOW WE ARE HUMAN, WE HAVE EMOTIONS, AND THAT WE LOVE OUR CHILD WHO DIED SO DEEPLY THAT WE SHOW EMOTIONS WHILE CONTROLLING THE LIGHTNING."

DEAR FELLOW DAD,

Welcome to a community to which none of us want to belong. Brought together by the disastrous loss of our children, a disparate group of individuals now forms a "we." Even if we don't want to speak, even if we can barely get out of bed, even if we have no clue how to proceed, we are nonetheless yoked together now and bear some responsibility for helping each other to continue living and living well.

My son Finlay died in the final hours of childbirth on June 5, 2014. Since then, I have devoted myself to grieving openly and to understanding what knowledge grief brings with it. Of the many things I have learned about myself, about my wife, about the nature of love, and about the pain of loss, the most important lesson bequeathed to me by Finlay has been to question the legitimacy of rules and customs. Certain rules, of course, keep us alive. We take it for granted that, when driving, our fellow motorists won't swerve across the yellow line. The rules of the road are quite real and useful. Likewise, the rule of cause and effect seems to persist and to insist that my son's death leads to an acute pain that I cannot ignore unless I want to make the pain worse. This rule teaches me that Finlay's death produces physical and psychological effects that are tangible and in need of repair. However, there are many rules that now reveal themselves as figments of the social imagination, and it is this set of rules that I believe we, as grieving fathers, should question as we heal. Perhaps we even need to question these rules in order to heal.

One rule that I find particularly important to question is the unspoken rule that men must be strong for their partners and themselves and that this strength requires an apathetic stoicism. This, I believe, is completely false. The social script that leads men to play the part of emotionless beings unfazed by the tremendous weight of a child's death is a script that we should lay aside. Also false is the assumption that women are necessarily more emotional than men and that men should "keep it together" while their partners "fall apart." Instead of following these rules blindly, I believe we are tasked with writing a new script for ourselves, one that motivates us to care for our bodies and minds, to care for the needs of our children's mothers, and to seek out a new definition of masculinity. What does strength look like when it is unaffiliated with profane muscularity? What are the benefits of opening to pain instead of sealing ourselves off from it? How might our relationships with our most intimate partners benefit from sharing in the healing process together? Answers to these questions come from challenging the readymade definitions of "male," "husband," and "dad" proffered by popular culture. Two years on from the death of my son, I am convinced that challenging such definitions leads to a new, more healthful life.

There are many other rules and questions that we must investigate as we grieve. I encourage you to seek them out actively. Of the many gifts left to us by our children, the gift of vision is the most powerful. In particular, the gift of a laser-like vision capable of cutting through the unimportant parts of our daily performances and laying bare the dimensions of life that truly matter. Seek out other Dads like us to help you in this quest, and let the love you feel for your child be the light that guides you along your way.

Sincerely,

Will Daddario

Father of Finlay Emilio Zerdy Daddario
Author of "To Grieve" (accessible here: http://www.performancephilosophy.org/journal/article/view/10/27)

*"ONE RULE THAT I FIND PARTICULARLY
IMPORTANT TO QUESTION IS THE
UNSPOKEN RULE THAT MEN MUST BE
STRONG FOR THEIR PARTNERS AND
THEMSELVES AND THAT THIS STRENGTH
REQUIRES AN APATHETIC STOICISM.
THIS, I BELIEVE, IS COMPLETELY FALSE.
INSTEAD OF FOLLOWING THESE RULES
BLINDLY, I BELIEVE WE ARE TASKED WITH
WRITING A NEW SCRIPT FOR OURSELVES,
ONE THAT MOTIVATES US TO CARE
FOR OUR BODIES AND MINDS, TO CARE
FOR THE NEEDS OF OUR CHILDREN'S
MOTHERS, AND TO SEEK OUT A NEW
DEFINITION OF MASCULINITY."*

DEAR FELLOW BEREAVED FATHER,

I'm sorry for your loss. There are no words I can say that will take the pain from losing your child away. No one should tell you any different.

Your pain is your pain alone and there are no set guidelines to how or how long you should grieve. The pain, the emptiness and the anger all show the love for your child. That love is never ending and is always present. Trying to hide your grief is like trying to hide the love you have for your child, no matter their age when they passed.

A little space, a little distance, and a chance to reconcile the dreadful feelings might be what's needed at this time. Make sure you find it for yourself as that's all that matters when you're facing this harsh "new reality".

People will tell you that after some period of time that you should be moving on. Well, there's no moving on or distancing yourself from your loss. Other parents who have not lost a child can't relate. Find others you can relate to as they offer only support and advice only when asked.

You learn to live with what life has dealt you and remember your child every day. In fact, now more than ever, memories are so important and extremely precious. It's these memories that keep you going and remind you of the bond you still have. It's a never "he or she was," but "he or she is," as they are still here in the present. You love them. You talk to them. They are still here. Past tense should never be in your vocabulary when describing your child and their connection to you.

Vacations, holidays and special family events will always be difficult. The memories of special times and continuing to incorporate your child into your new life is possible and also important. Try putting their pictures at the Thanksgiving or Christmas table, take them with you on vacation and celebrate birthdays. Most people understand and appreciate this.

Other people will also talk about healing and finding joy. Yes, you learn to live and laugh, but pure joy again is ever evading. The hole that's underneath is always there. Don't try to avoid it or fill it in. You'll learn to navigate it, but not hide it from it.

No matter what, you will always love your child. That precious love and gift given to us will always remain. Hold your head high for keeping the love and balance your broken heart. That blending, as strange as it sounds, has worked for me.

-- *Tom Mitchell*

Father to Drew Mitchell

"NO MATTER WHAT, YOU WILL ALWAYS LOVE YOUR CHILD. THAT PRECIOUS LOVE AND GIFT GIVEN TO US WILL ALWAYS REMAIN. HOLD YOUR HEAD HIGH FOR KEEPING THE LOVE AND BALANCE YOUR BROKEN HEART. THAT BLENDING, AS STRANGE AS IT SOUNDS, HAS WORKED FOR ME."

DEAR FATHER AND FRIEND IN SORROW,

It is important for me to start this letter by telling you what I wish others would have understood when my son passed away: I do not understand what you are going through, I do not know what it feels like, and I cannot help you get over it. No matter how similar our circumstances might be, I am not you… I do not cope the way you do… I do not feel what you feel.

I want you to know that people will come along, with all of the right intentions, and offer you all the wise and comforting words in the world and the only advice I can really give you is… it's okay. It's okay to be mad, it's okay to be sad, it's okay to not want to talk about it. It's even okay to want to hit those who think they "understand you and what you are going through." It's okay to go back to work and continue on with your life as "normal" to help soften the hole in your heart. It's okay to feel like everyone cares about "mommy" and no one really wants to understand how "daddy" is feeling. You don't have to cry to grieve, you don't have to act any way that anyone says you should. It is even okay to get mad at God and ask Him why; He understands.

It is okay.

With all that being said, if you are reading this, you are most likely looking me to tell you something that might be helpful to you in your moment of need and emotional pain. Well, based solely on what I experienced August 7, 2008 when my son passed away, perhaps I can help you out a little by sharing with you what I know helped me. Perhaps in it, you can find something that can help you as you soldier on.

It will never "get better," but it will get easier to manage the emotions. When you find that friend with whom you can sit in a golf cart, or on a fishing boat, or on the back porch, or in a pub, and just be there, silent, with no words exchanged and they don't try to "coach you" or "explain why this happened" but can just sit there and be your friend, you will find in those moments of silent friendship a calm. Those brief moments of calm helped me realize that I am not alone; that while my friend cannot understand what I am feeling, he cares enough to be willing to sit almost uncomfortably quiet and be there with me. If I can encourage you at all, to do anything, it would be to find that friend.

The freedom for you is not in the release or the acceptance or the scheduled program of grief, but in your ability to give yourself permission to feel and to, at times, be irrational. There is nothing in life that can prepare you to handle what you are going to experience, so let yourself off the hook and don't try to box yourself into the stereotypes of manly emotions. If you feel like crying, cry. If you feel like yelling, yell. Do whatever you need to and do not hold it in. Your freedom to grieve how you grieve is the one thing you should never take away from yourself.

Let the world say what it wants, let the experts talk, let your wife or partner get all the attention from the other ladies… you made your life and your job what it is, now go make your grief be what you need it to be and find a friend so connected to you that he knows the best thing he can say sometimes… is nothing.

- Sam Rodriguez

Father of Manuel Michael Rodriguez
http://www.facebook.com/mannysfund

"THERE IS NOTHING IN LIFE THAT CAN PREPARE YOU TO HANDLE WHAT YOU ARE GOING TO EXPERIENCE, SO LET YOURSELF OFF THE HOOK AND DON'T TRY TO BOX YOURSELF INTO THE STEREOTYPES OF MANLY EMOTIONS. IF YOU FEEL LIKE CRYING, CRY. IF YOU FEEL LIKE YELLING, YELL. DO WHATEVER YOU NEED TO AND DO NOT HOLD IT IN. YOUR FREEDOM TO GRIEVE HOW YOU GRIEVE IS THE ONE THING YOU SHOULD NEVER TAKE AWAY FROM YOURSELF."

FATHERS,

On October 25th of last year I lost my best friend in the world, my 27-year-old son. We did pretty much everything together; playing sports, fishing, working out, hanging out and watching lots of college football. In his early 20's he started suffering from what I would call severe OCD. He always had a minor issue with the disease, but it never really seemed to be anything to worry about until it hit him hard. To add insult to injury he was prescribed opiates to control back pain as a result of some torn lower discs that he had from a weight lifting issue. He became highly addicted to the opiates as they not only blocked his pain but also turned the racing thoughts in his mind off, something that the other anti-anxiety drugs he was prescribed could not do. Little did I know that this would eventually kill him. We were supposed to go to the gym the morning I found him dead in his bed with his alarm going off. His death was ruled an accidental opiate overdose. My life from that moment on, as did his mother's and 25-year-old sister's, changed to something unimaginable.

To all of you fathers that have lost sons or daughters, I am so very sorry that any of us are a part of this hell on earth. I do, however, want to stress that as hard as it seems, life really does go on and you have to be a part of it. You will have days when you can't get out of bed and you will think about things that you once thought important differently, but you must live life for your remaining loved ones. They will need you more than ever. You also need to try and just be strong for yourself… easier said than done I know! I believe that fathers hurt just as bad as mothers when they lose a child and I wish I had some magical words of comfort for you fellow dads out there. I am finding, as many people say, that time is the real healer. Since Robby passed on I have heard so many different stories of families losing children for so many different reasons and though I can't feel exactly how every one of you do, I can say that this grief, this pain was never meant for us to have to endure. It will truly test our strength, our faith and all things we once thought to matter in this world.

We don't know why these things happen to us and our children, but for me knowing that I will see him again one day makes life bearable. I believe it really is not the end, just the end here on earth and that this life we are living now is but an instant. What I wouldn't give though to hold him and tell how much I love him just one more time.

Another thing that has helped me is to talk to other dads that have lost children. Just to have someone listen to you who actually knows how you feel and for you to know how they feel. It helps you to not feel so isolated and alone. About

2 months after my son died my wife and I started going to an organization called "TCF" (The Compassionate Friends) which is a worldwide organization for parents and siblings of lost sons and daughters that can be found online and helps to deal with the grief in a setting where we all can share our thoughts. They normally have local chapters that you can attend monthly meetings. I wish all of you dads peace of mind. Bless you and your families.

Rob

Rob Williams, Orlando, FL

*"WE DON'T KNOW WHY THESE THINGS
HAPPEN TO US AND OUR CHILDREN, BUT
FOR ME KNOWING THAT I WILL SEE HIM
AGAIN ONE DAY MAKES LIFE BEARABLE.
I BELIEVE IT REALLY IS NOT THE END,
JUST THE END HERE ON EARTH AND THAT
THIS LIFE WE ARE LIVING NOW IS BUT AN
INSTANT. WHAT I WOULDN'T GIVE THOUGH
TO HOLD HIM AND TELL HOW MUCH I
LOVE HIM JUST ONE MORE TIME."*

DEAR FATHER,

I contemplate what to write to support you through the
most difficult experience of your life and I come up empty.
I am empty because I know there are no words to comfort
you, there is no insight to take the pain away and, most of
all, there is nothing that will bring your child back. So, I am
empty, left only with the experience of Zeek's miscarriage
followed by Carwyn's stillbirth. I have found myself
staggering through the emptiness searching for meaning.
Trying to find the answers to the whys and the hows but
nothing comes. I continue to swim through the mysteries
and horrors of my soul and a few truths have bubbled up. The
truths are the glue that has held me together and allowed me
to continue on my path of grieving. At this point there are
three basic truths I believe about the experience of losing a
child.

1. The experience will break you

2. Your path of grief is for you to walk alone

3. You will be ok

Following Carwyn's stillbirth, I remember a lot of people
tell me to "be strong," "hold it together," "you can beat
this," and I ignored their words. Through this experience I
continue to realize how the messages our society sends males

is damaging. Events like this are meant to break us. They are intended to shatter our worlds so that we can collect the pieces and recreate ourselves. They offer us the opportunity to reconstruct ourselves from the core out. In the hospital, my wife Erica and I were discussing how we would survive and I remember telling her, "we will fall apart together." Allowing the experience to break you is not a sign of weakness, instead it is a sign you are fully alive.

There is no way to examine the grieving process that allows it to be predictable, categorized, or even understood. All the material I have read leads me to believe that when this is done to grief, you make it sterile and not helpful. Grief is a human experience that is ultimately about love, and like love we all experience grief individually. What causes me pain through the process is helpful to another and what helps me enrages someone else. This leads me to a place of understanding that my path of grief is for me to walk alone. My path of grief will lead me to my spiritual emergence, like yours will lead you to yours.

The last truth is the most difficult for me to write to you about. This is because depending on the day, the hour, or the minute I may **or may not beli**eve it myself. There are moments when I am able to see some benefit from the stillbirth and there are other times when I am left paralyzed on the floor from the pain. There are flashes when I am able to connect to the outside world and then I fall back into the bottomless pit of my soul. There are times when I hold the hope for my family, and then there are times when I have to trust what my five-year-old daughter tells me when she looks me in the eyes and says, "It will be ok, Daddy."

Reid Smithdeal

Zeek and Carwyn's daddy

"THE EXPERIENCE WILL BREAK YOU

YOUR PATH OF GRIEF IS FOR YOU TO WALK
ALONE

YOU WILL BE OK"

FATHERS,

I know faith has been important to help me and my family
heal from the passing away of Pierce Allen. I don't want to
push faith onto the reader of this but relying on your faith is
extremely important. The explanation of why your situation
occurred will drive you crazy, but use faith to heal, knowing
that your loved one has reached a better place.

Pierce Allen Cartwright was born on May 22, 2009 and went
to heaven on May 25, 2013. He had just turned four with a
lifetime of love and fun in front of him. Pierce was all boy,
into everything and wanting to help. Pierce loved the cartoon
Umizoomi, his John Deere power wheel gator, and Mickey
Mouse. He is loved and missed dearly by all who knew him.

Since Pierce wanted to help and often walked around the
house with his toy doctor bag calling himself "Doctor Pierce,"
we have tried to remember him and build a legacy of helping
others under his name. On the way home from the hospital
on that May day that we can't forget about, we received a call
from the Mississippi Organ Recovery Agency (M.O.R.A.)
asking if we were interested in allowing Pierce to be an organ
/ tissue donor. My wife immediately said "Yes!!" then asked
me if that was okay. I was completely okay with that decision
because Pierce wanted to help. This way he could continue to

help someone, somehow, someday. M.O.R.A. recovered his heart values. This decision to allow Pierce to become a tissue donor was one of the easiest and most rewarding decisions I have ever made in my life. Also, to continue Pierce's helping spirit, my wife and I have organized the Pierce Allen Community Day and Memorial Blood Drive. We wanted a way for people to learn about different outreach groups along the Mississippi Gulf Coast who were here to help them. I am a teacher and now I sponsor a community service group at the school. We raise items and/or money to help different groups in the community. My wife and I buy school supplies every year for the grade Pierce would be in and then donate the supplies to a teacher to help students that can't afford them.

I mention all the ways we carry on Pierce's desire to help as a way to explain that there is no right or wrong way to grieve for your loved one. You need to grieve, but I would stress to you to find a positive outlet for your mind, body, and emotions. It is far more rewarding to look back and see all the positives that have happened as a way to remember your loved one instead of the possible negatives. I would rather have Pierce with us, but since I can't, I will carry him on through positive acts of helping others for him.

The "new normal" you experience will suck and it is hard to adjust to. At first there are people around that temporarily distract you from your situation, but once they are gone it gets dark and lonely. You have to look around to find a positive outlet. People will try not to act differently, but they will. They won't know what to say or do so they will act differently and say some dumb stuff to you in an attempt to help. Try not to let this bother you too much even though it is tough to not let it get under your skin. People will want to talk about your loved one, but not know how to bring them up. I love talking about Pierce, hearing others talk about Pierce, and watching videos of him. It is tough but he is being talked about and isn't forgotten.

As a male we are told not to cry and to be tough. Well, that is a bunch of crap. Be emotional. Cry if you need to cry. It is a healthy way to handle your emotions. You need to get the emotions out. You can't keep it bottled up. I understand maybe you have kids and/or a spouse around and you might want to be there and be tough for them, but find time for you to cope with what you're feeling. This took me a long time to figure out. I was trying to keep things deep down inside and I didn't deal well with my emotions because guys don't cry. I didn't want my wife and sons to see me so upset because they needed me. Eventually, I had to deal with Pierce's ascent to heaven and how I felt inside. In hindsight, me handling my emotions has allowed me to help my family more. You are human, you have to process the emotions and events around you.

People will watch how you cope with this tragedy and the effects will reach deeper and wider than you might realize at first. I knew I had to be strong and supportive for my other sons and wife but what I didn't realize was the effects on grandparents, great grandparents, uncles, aunts, cousins, co-workers, and friends. It affected people who have read about Pierce's life and the events afterwards. They all have been changed one way or another. I hope for Pierce there is more good than bad to see as he watches over us from up above.

At four years old, Pierce was gone before his true impact on the town, county, state, country, and maybe the world could truly be felt. I hope, pray, and plan to leave a legacy of positive for Pierce Allen because from the moment he was born, he changed me. I want people to feel how he could have been the positive change they needed in their life too.

Matthew Cartwright
Father of Pierce Allen

"AS A MALE WE ARE TOLD NOT TO CRY AND TO BE TOUGH. WELL, THAT IS A BUNCH OF CRAP. BE EMOTIONAL. CRY IF YOU NEED TO CRY. IT IS A HEALTHY WAY TO HANDLE YOUR EMOTIONS. YOU NEED TO GET THE EMOTIONS OUT. YOU CAN'T KEEP IT BOTTLED UP. I UNDERSTAND MAYBE YOU HAVE KIDS AND/OR A SPOUSE AROUND AND YOU MIGHT WANT TO BE THERE AND BE TOUGH FOR THEM, BUT FIND TIME FOR YOU TO COPE WITH WHAT YOU'RE FEELING."

DEAR FELLOW FATHER,

First and foremost, I am sorry to hear of your loss. In 2015, my wife and I lost our son a few hours after birth. I know my story will not make your situation any easier to deal with, but I want you to know that you do not walk this journey alone.

As I look back on my journey, there are a few things that I wish I would have known. I hope some of the lessons that I learned along the way will help you as you face this battle.

Talk about your loss with those who are open to talking about it. Keeping your feelings inside will only make the pain greater. I found that talking with others who experienced a similar type of loss was the best way to cope with my feelings. Many people will try to help and will offer comforting words, but as hard as they try, they just don't understand how this feels. If there isn't someone to talk to or you just aren't up for talking about it yet, write regularly in a journal. I found that getting my feelings out, whether spoken aloud or written on paper was very beneficial.

Keep an open line of communication with your significant other. Know that you will both grieve differently. One day she may be sad when you are not. That is okay, it is normal. Everyone grieves differently. It doesn't mean you care any less than she does. Be there for her when she needs you.

Some people you meet will be uncomfortable talking about your loss. Don't fault them for that. Everyone deals with emotions differently. For every person that you meet who doesn't want to talk about the loss of your child, you will find someone that wants to clear their calendar to be with you when you need it.

Take time for yourself. You have been through a lot physically, mentally and emotionally. Recovering from that is neither quick or easy. You may have trouble sleeping and your motivation to exercise and take care of yourself may decrease. Getting back into a routine may be tough, but over time you will get back into the swing of things.

Give yourself permission to grieve. Don't let anyone tell you how to grieve or how long the grieving process should last. No two people deal with loss the same. The loss of my son is something I will never let go of. I honor his legacy by sharing his story.

A lot of people will tell you that it gets easier over time. I don't necessarily agree. The pain doesn't go away, but over time life provides us with distractions that make some days easier than others. There are still days that hurt more than others. Birthdays, holidays and other anniversaries are particularly tough.

I wish I could tell you this journey will be easy. Unfortunately, it won't be. What I can tell you is that the worst days are already behind you. You made it this far and that is an accomplishment to be proud of. I hope that you find comfort and healing in the days that lie ahead.

Regards,

Kevin Evers

Father of Noah Anthony Evers
www.AFatherOfLoss.com

*"GIVE YOURSELF PERMISSION TO GRIEVE.
DON'T LET ANYONE TELL YOU HOW TO
GRIEVE OR HOW LONG THE GRIEVING
PROCESS SHOULD LAST. NO TWO PEOPLE
DEAL WITH LOSS THE SAME. THE LOSS OF
MY SON IS SOMETHING I WILL NEVER LET
GO OF. I HONOR HIS LEGACY BY SHARING
HIS STORY."*

TO ALL FATHERS WHO HAVE ALSO LOST A CHILD,

My son's name is Asher.

My wife, Betsy, and I were beyond excited when we discovered that we were expecting our first child. Everything was going smoothly. We had no medical issues, he was growing in a healthy manner, he had all 10 fingers and toes—our baby was perfect.

On April 11, 2016, my whole life changed. I got a phone call at work from Betsy telling me that Asher made a really big movement, then stopped. She was concerned, so I told her to go into the local women's health office to check up on him. I wasn't worried until she called back. My heart broke when she gave me the news that our baby—our first and only child—was gone. I immediately left work to be with her. I barely remember the 30 minutes of travel to get to her.

After some time to discuss what would happen next (a process that wasn't supposed to happen), we called our relatives to deliver the news—conversations that will forever be seared into my memory. We prepared our things and went to the hospital to prepare for the cesarean section. The hospital staff was phenomenal and made it the best bad experience that it could be.

Asher was born. The umbilical cord had a tight knot in it and it was wrapped around his neck three times. My son's death was quick and painless. For his whole life, he knew no pain, only warmth and love. He was—and will always be—perfect.

My in-laws drove in from Ohio, Betsy's sisters flew in from California and Illinois, my parents and sisters came from home near Betsy and me. Our whole family was with us in those worst of times. We supported each other, cried together, hugged, mourned, and reflected together.

We had Asher with us for 29 hours after his birth. We took pictures of him, held him, sang to him, read to him, and loved him with everything we had in our hearts to give. At the 29th hour, we knew that the time had come to do the hardest thing we have ever (and probably will ever) do in our lives— say goodbye.

Asher is now cremated and sits on our piano so he can always hear the music Betsy plays. He is a constant presence in our lives and we love him dearly.

I tell you all of this to share Asher's story. Your story is different. Tell your child's story. I bring Asher up in conversation frequently. The more I talk about him, the more alive and present he feels to me. There are times when he feels like a distant memory, though he was with us only months prior to the writing of this letter. Telling his story is always fresh and brings him to the forefront of our minds.

In these times, you will feel a plethora of things. I encourage you to feel them all fully. At no point over the course of my grief have I felt guilty for not feeling the things the way that I should. There are times to feel immense sorrow—cry whenever you need to. There are times to feel happiness— smile and laugh. There are times to feel angry—be angry in a productive way. There are times to feel lost—find someone to be lost with you or to help guide you home. Sometimes you even feel conflicting emotions simultaneously. All emotions are valid in grief.

The hope is that eventually, you will be able to find some contentment and acceptance. I am not there yet. Some days are better than others, but I feel that I am on the right road to acceptance because I am feeling what my mind and body are telling me to feel and covering nothing up.

Betsy and I communicate effectively all the time. We have made the conscious decision to talk about what we are feeling and thoughts we are having. That open line of communication has fortified our trust in each other. When we are sad, we make a point of letting the other know so we can be whatever kind of support is needed at that moment. When we are happy, we share in that together. If you feel uncomfortable with sharing out loud, I encourage you to find a way to still communicate. I have been told by multiple couples who have lost a child that keeping a journal that the other person can read whenever they need to has saved their relationship. Do not let your relationship with your partner die because it is challenging to communicate. Find a method that works for you.

I also journal frequently. I never journaled before we lost Asher. When he passed though, I knew that I didn't want to forget any part of his life, any important feelings I have, or any other event that is relevant to him and his story. I have written down every bit of his existence on this Earth outside of his mother's womb. I cherish the words that I wrote. I have preserved the memories I never want to forget.

My last bit of advice for you, my friend, is to find the silver linings in your life. Count your blessings. Literally count your blessings. Find all of the good things in your life because some days you will need to remember them. Some days your life will feel pointless and devoid of love, but the silver linings in your life will remind you that it is not all bad. You can make it through this. You will make it through this. Your life will improve. You will never forget your son or daughter. You will never stop grieving. But you will one day be happy that he or she was in your life, albeit for too short of a time.

Be strong, but only when you need to be strong. Be weak, but only when you need to be weak. Cry, but only when you need to cry. Smile, but only when you need to smile. Love your child. Always.

Many blessings to you and comfort in your time of need,

Kavin Ley

Father of Asher

"Too Wonderful (Asher's Song)" https://www.youtube.com/watch?v=xnLcTc0rUzg

"MY LAST BIT OF ADVICE FOR YOU, MY FRIEND, IS TO FIND THE SILVER LININGS IN YOUR LIFE. COUNT YOUR BLESSINGS. *LITERALLY* COUNT YOUR BLESSINGS. FIND ALL OF THE GOOD THINGS IN YOUR LIFE BECAUSE SOME DAYS YOU WILL NEED TO REMEMBER THEM. SOME DAYS YOUR LIFE WILL FEEL POINTLESS AND DEVOID OF LOVE, BUT THE SILVER LININGS IN YOUR LIFE WILL REMIND YOU THAT IT IS NOT ALL BAD. YOU CAN MAKE IT THROUGH THIS. YOU WILL MAKE IT THROUGH THIS. YOUR LIFE WILL IMPROVE. YOU WILL NEVER FORGET YOUR SON OR DAUGHTER. YOU WILL NEVER STOP GRIEVING. BUT YOU WILL ONE DAY BE HAPPY THAT HE OR SHE WAS IN YOUR LIFE, ALBEIT FOR TOO SHORT OF A TIME."

JUNE 29TH, 2013

It was a normal Friday; we were just finishing up dinner and had plans to meet with out of town friends when my wife began to feel a little off. Thinking nothing of it, she took some antacids and went to lie down. Everything happened so fast, less than 12 hours later, we had to deliver our daughter, Collins Victoria Moffatt, by emergency C-section at 25 weeks gestation. My wife had developed HELLP Syndrome and was losing her life. Sadly, Collins was too under-developed to survive. I stood in the operating room, crying, holding my daughter, looking at my wife not knowing if she was going to survive.

As my wife's condition remained critical and they decided to transport her to a larger hospital. As they prepped her for travel, I kissed Collins' forehead, and said goodbye.

When we arrived, my wife was still in a medically induced coma which was necessary to keep her vitals stable. I remember sitting by my wife's bed, trying to think of a way to tell her our daughter didn't survive. As she woke up, she looked into my eyes and asked the question I hoped she wouldn't for a while - Where's Collins? I told her what had happened. She just stared at me, not able to process what I was actually saying. The one person I needed to console me, who had been there for me through every hardship, could not comprehend the situation. Did I tell her too soon? Should I have waited until she was more coherent? Should I have lied and told her Collins was going to be okay? It wasn't until the next few days that she started understanding what had happened.

Once we returned home, we had the difficult task of making final arrangements for our daughter, while still dealing with the emotional and physical pain. Being from a smaller community where there isn't a lot of resources for families who lose a child, my wife and I relied on each other for the first little while. There were sleepless nights, questions with no answers, and moments of complete breakdowns. If we didn't have each other, I don't know what would have happened. We eventually found other people through social media who had dealt with a similar loss, and continue to be a support system to each other. It's comforting to know other people who are feeling the same way you are, and to put some normalcy into the situation.

One thing I have learned is never be afraid to talk about your child. It doesn't mean you have to bring them up with every person you meet, but if you find someone you have a bond with, talk about your child. Share your story, because you never know who it might help. I find that the more I talk about Collins the easier it gets, and I have had other people open up to me for the very first time about their loss.

We now have a beautiful 2-year-old daughter. We have told her about Collins, and are very open about her having a sister in heaven. I'm not religious, but I do like to believe there is something after life ends. That's why every year on Collins birthday, June 30th, the three of us gather at a special spot, write letters and send them up on a balloon. It's our way of letting her know we still think about her and will continue to for the rest of our lives.

Jonathan Moffitt

Father of Collins Victoria Moffitt

"ONE THING I HAVE LEARNED IS NEVER BE AFRAID TO TALK ABOUT YOUR CHILD. IT DOESN'T MEAN YOU HAVE TO BRING THEM UP WITH EVERY PERSON YOU MEET, BUT IF YOU FIND SOMEONE YOU HAVE A BOND WITH, TALK ABOUT YOUR CHILD. SHARE YOUR STORY, BECAUSE YOU NEVER KNOW WHO IT MIGHT HELP. I FIND THAT THE MORE I TALK ABOUT COLLINS THE EASIER IT GETS, AND I HAVE HAD OTHER PEOPLE OPEN UP TO ME FOR THE VERY FIRST TIME ABOUT THEIR LOSS."

DEAR FATHERS,

My wife and I met later in life, married at 32 and tried
to have a family for a number of years without success.
Eventually I began expecting to become one of those couples
in your life, together forever but no children and you never
really ask why. I have a few in my life. We were more than a
little surprised when, at age 41, it happened and suddenly we
were going to be a completely different couple, an older but
ecstatic pair of parents. The pregnancy had concerns, but none
that serious. We recorded milestones and prepared our home
and our lives for the transformative event.

Days after my wife's birthday, right within her expectancy
period, we attended our last doctor visit, and made plans to
induce after the weekend if nothing progressed naturally.
During the night, a velamentous umbilical cord detached, and
my daughter died. My wife woke early, felt no activity, and off
to the hospital we went, where the doctor informed us there
was no heartbeat. The worst day of my life.

I am not religious, though I can understand how that might
offer comfort, but I was not before her stillbirth and will
not take it up after. Everywhere we looked after we returned
home was a reminder of a life that wasn't ours anymore. We
had other tasks, paperwork and burial plots. Our extended
family came to aid however they could, but there was a

feeling of emptiness, pain, loss, depression and failure. Time healed, as far as beginning to be a functional person in society, but there were daily reminders of what we weren't and what we were. A number of older couples approached us privately, and shared similar stories from a previous generation, where they often didn't even hold their child, as that was a standard practice that has gladly become phased away. The approximately 30 hours we spent with Anja are all we had and will ever have, and I am grateful for them. It's all we get with her.

People throughout history have suffered this tragedy, some many more times than us. I sometimes think of the more well-known examples and feel a kinship in the world's worst club I can think of. My wife and I adopted a little boy two years later, whose birthday fell one day after our daughter's, and he is a source of joy as he grows older, but this is counterbalanced by any person kindly asking "Is he your only child?" What can you say? You develop responses, whether it's someone you deem worth opening up to, or whether you don't or you speak without considering that equation. I try to mention her when I can, she's my daughter and that's all I can do for her.

If there is one thing I can pass on, even though you might feel it or even wish it, you aren't alone.

Jason Satek

Father of Anja

IF THERE IS ONE THING I CAN PASS ON,
EVEN THOUGH YOU MIGHT FEEL IT OR
EVEN WISH IT, YOU AREN'T ALONE.

MY FRIEND, I AM SO SORRY.

I hate this for you, so much. I feel your pain. You are not alone, even though it feels like you are right now.

Know this, you will get through it. You will make it to the other side. It doesn't feel like it right now, but you will. Right now, you feel sick. You feel like you have been punched in the gut. It hurts to breathe, but you will make it.

Right now, you are in the depths of the worst pain imaginable. This pain, the pain of losing a child, or children, is the worst pain there could possibly be. It's one thing to lose a grandparent, or a parent, but to lose a child, that isn't how this world is supposed to work. When my father passed away, as I walked my grandfather into the funeral home, my grandfather said, "You never think you're going to have bury your own child." I agreed with him, but didn't understand the depths of that pain until 2 years later, when I said goodbye to two of my own children.

I know as males, we are reluctant to show emotion, especially in public, but it's okay. You have to get it out. It's grief. It's the process we go through. Showing emotion isn't being weak. Showing emotion isn't not being there for your wife. Showing emotion is grief.

Your wife needs you. She is feeling all of the same pain you are, and perhaps even compounded with guilt. While you feel weak and vulnerable, you still have to be there for her. Go through this process with her, you are a team. Cling to each other. Love each other. Grow stronger in your relationship. You WILL make it through this, as much as it doesn't feel like it.

If you are religious, cling to that as well. However, know it is okay to be angry. It's okay to yell. It's okay to doubt. Along with your marriage, grow stronger in your faith through this.

Remember your child or children. Don't be afraid to show pictures. Don't be afraid to talk about your child or children. You are a dad! You will always be a dad. Don't let anyone take that from you, or diminish the importance of the time your child(ren) was here on earth, whether that child ever took a breath outside of the womb or not. Your child(ren) matters! You are their father, you are!

This phase you are in will eventually pass. This immense pain will gradually begin to ease. However; there will still be days when it hits you all over again. That's okay! You will find a new normal, and you will get through this storm.

May God Bless You and Yours.

Dusty Hurst

Father to Angel Twins Chandler Charles & Paisley Joan

"I KNOW AS MALES, WE ARE RELUCTANT TO SHOW EMOTION, ESPECIALLY IN PUBLIC, BUT IT'S OKAY. YOU HAVE TO GET IT OUT. IT'S GRIEF. IT'S THE PROCESS WE GO THROUGH. SHOWING EMOTION ISN'T BEING WEAK. SHOWING EMOTION ISN'T NOT BEING THERE FOR YOUR WIFE. SHOWING EMOTION IS GRIEF."

TO WHOM IT MAY CONCERN:

It occurs to me that one of my guiding beliefs is that no man should tell another how to live his life. So, I'm not saying what you should or should not do, or what you should or should not feel. This is my story, and Maty's. Yours, I guess, is similar. There is light past the darkness, but there is also darkness in that light.

There's a lot to say about the death of my son, and about his life, and about what all of that means to me. Boiling that down to a few paragraphs is difficult. This letter is to a father who is going to live on past the death of his child, so I'll try to focus on that aspect of the story.

After 12 years of marriage, my wife and I won the kid lottery. Really, our odds of conception were that low. We even referred to our not having a biological child as a "loss". Forgive us, we were naive.

The pregnancy went well, until it didn't. For many reasons, both moral and medical, abortion was not an option. Bad news trickled down on us a bit at a time for months until the gravity of the situation was finally undeniable to the doctors and to us. With each check-up, it fell to me to lie to my wife as she cried in my arms in the hospital parking lot.

In the beginning, I lied to both of us that I wasn't worried. Later I lied to both of us that there was "always hope." If Maty had been a girl, her name would have been Hope. When my wife cried, I held her and tried to cry with her.

I'll share that my son, Matthew, was born on July 17, 2014 and died two hours after his birth. We made the difficult decision not to pursue extreme measures to prolong his life as his condition was terminal and it would have been selfish of us to cause him that pain. My wife and I held our son, sang to him, and rocked him for his entire life.

The problem for me is that I get angry. My wife asks what she did wrong or "why us?" I just get angry and want to hit a wall or throw something. When I was alone I would scream to God.

Women tend to insist that men talk things out the way that they do or look to God or to the afterlife for solace. That type of thinking only reminds me of what I've lost and makes me angry. I had to learn to grieve with her for as long as I could, but then to say that I simply cannot take any more for a while.

I had to let her know that my grieving process was different from hers. If I'm drinking a cup of coffee on my front porch and watching the rain pour down, I'm grieving. I'm trying to recover. I'm trying to heal. I will focus on the beauty of nature around me and remind myself that there is still good in the world. It's a moment by moment thing. I know that I will never be care-free again, and have no hope of unabashed joy in my heart. It's sad, but true. The best I can hope for are a few moments of appreciation of what is good.

Respecting each other's differences in the grieving process saved our marriage.

Life is beautiful, but difficult and unfair.

Maty's Daddy

"IF I'M DRINKING A CUP OF COFFEE ON MY FRONT PORCH AND WATCHING THE RAIN POUR DOWN, I'M GRIEVING. I'M TRYING TO RECOVER. I'M TRYING TO HEAL. I WILL FOCUS ON THE BEAUTY OF NATURE AROUND ME AND REMIND MYSELF THAT THERE IS STILL GOOD IN THE WORLD. IT'S A MOMENT BY MOMENT THING. I KNOW THAT I WILL NEVER BE CARE-FREE AGAIN, AND HAVE NO HOPE OF UNABASHED JOY IN MY HEART. IT'S SAD, BUT TRUE. THE BEST I CAN HOPE FOR ARE A FEW MOMENTS OF APPRECIATION OF WHAT IS GOOD."

DEAR DAD,

I am writing this letter to you, although I don't know you and you don't know me. But that doesn't matter because we are connected by something that is very deep and very powerful – the death of our child. I will not tell you how to feel, I will not presume to know exactly how you feel. But I can tell you how I felt and how I feel now after 4 and a half years.

If you were like me, you spent a long time getting ready to be a dad, you had hopes and dreams for your child. You imagined what it would be like holding their hands while they take their first steps, you recounted the imaginary steps to some imaginary school on their first day, you imagined how you would teach them to ride a bike. Now it is almost as if everything was just in your imagination.

If you were like me, you will feel that everyone has moved on quickly and that everyone has forgotten and moved on with their lives. It feels like your friends and family have betrayed not just you, but the memory of your child. You may even think this of your partner. I think this is an important message - you and your partner will be in different places in grief. It sounds ridiculous, but grief is a journey to a destination that does not exist. The journey continues and never seems to change, but believe me, things do change. It might be hard with your partner at times, but together you are stronger, I have no doubt.

If you are like me, you will never feel and think the same about the world as you did. It will feel more dangerous, darker and more profoundly unfair. Your friends and family will complain about their own children keeping them awake and you wish your child was crying and keeping you awake instead of the nightmares of their death. Your friends and family will accidentally say the stupidest of things. "It was God's plan," "God wanted an angel," "Everything happens for a reason," were the common things that I heard. You may lose friends, but those you will gain are perhaps some of the strongest bonds with people that you will ever know.

What will happen is that you will find a new normal, you will feel a new outlook that many people will not understand. Many people are scared of death and cannot accept that it happens to children, to babies. In the darkness that is ahead, there is a new light that you cannot see, but I can tell you that it is there. The new normal to you now might feel like a scary place that you don't want to be, and that is ok. I think that that is part of the process.

Four and a half years later, I can still remember the day that I held my daughter, stillborn two days after her due date. I held her in silence wishing that she would just take a single breath. Wishing that she would open her eyes and look at me. She didn't, but I am still her father and even though she never saw me, she knew I was there – she could hear me speak to her and to her mum, she could feel me when I ran my hand over her mum's stomach. I am still her dad, and even though my relationship with my daughter is not how I wanted it to be and even though she is dead, she is still my daughter and your child is still yours.

Your child had an impact on the world, you might not feel it, but they did. Like me you are a parent with a child who has died - those words are hard to read, to write, and even harder to say. But now as a parent you carry their memory into the future, a burden and delight.

I know you do not want to read a lot, I know that you don't want rambling. Just know that you are still you, a new you perhaps. And most importantly you are not alone.

In memory of mine and your child.

Marty

Father of Maya Alexandra Stephenson
http://maya.stephenson.muchloved.com

*"YOUR CHILD HAD AN IMPACT ON THE
WORLD, YOU MIGHT NOT FEEL IT, BUT
THEY DID. LIKE ME YOU ARE A PARENT
WITH A CHILD WHO HAS DIED - THOSE
WORDS ARE HARD TO READ, TO WRITE,
AND EVEN HARDER TO SAY. BUT NOW AS A
PARENT YOU CARRY THEIR MEMORY INTO
THE FUTURE, A BURDEN AND DELIGHT."*

DEAR GRIEVING DAD,

My daughter died, we found out we could not have any healthy children of our own, and the adoption of our daughter fell through just a few days before we went to court to finalize the adoption. We had 3 major losses in a very short period of time. I was extremely angry after all this. Why would God allow this to happen? Why did we keep having such terrible things happen to us? Those are questions I was asking after all this. I still don't have an answer for these questions. But one thing I do know is God still loves you and me. He still wants a relationship with us. It's ok to be angry at him. The Bible is filled with people that were angry at God at times. Just don't shut him out. He doesn't want a fake relationship. He wants a REAL relationship. Ask him questions, even yell at him, but keep talking to him.

I still don't have any more kids. Will I ever? I hope so but I don't know. I've learned life REALLY sucks sometimes. God doesn't always cause the bad things to happen, sometimes they just do. One thing I know for sure is God still loves you. He wants to hold you through it all. Don't ever give up on God. Don't turn your back on him. Run to him.

After all of this, my wife and I nearly got divorced. We were fighting a lot and there were many times I did not know if we were going to make it. I wasn't the husband my wife needed.

I didn't handle certain situations the way I should have. Grief and loss of someone you care about magnifies even the smallest issue, or the smallest flaw. Sometimes, out of her pain, your wife might lash out at you. Don't take it personally. Don't hold it against her. This is the time she needs you the most. Hold her extra tight and show her extra love. Forgive her and realize it's not her talking but the grief. That is the only way the two of you can make it through this. People grieve differently. People react differently and feel different emotions. They express themselves differently and need different things. It's ok if you feel something different than your wife, or something else helps you deal with the grief. What is good for you might not be good for her and vice versa. And that is ok. We are all different people. But don't ever give up on your wife. Keep fighting, keep forgiving, keep pushing through. If you are able to make it to the other side still together, your relationship will be that much stronger. Keep fighting.

Sincerely,

Another grieving father

"PEOPLE GRIEVE DIFFERENTLY. PEOPLE REACT DIFFERENTLY AND FEEL DIFFERENT EMOTIONS. THEY EXPRESS THEMSELVES DIFFERENTLY AND NEED DIFFERENT THINGS. IT'S OK IF YOU FEEL SOMETHING DIFFERENT THAN YOUR WIFE, OR SOMETHING ELSE HELPS YOU DEAL WITH THE GRIEF. WHAT IS GOOD FOR YOU MIGHT NOT BE GOOD FOR HER AND VICE VERSA. AND THAT IS OK. WE ARE ALL DIFFERENT PEOPLE."

A FATHER'S LOSS

Unfortunately, you're reading this for a reason that's just wrong, just as I am writing it for a reason that's just wrong. Wrong in the sense that we should never have to go through this. Wrong in the sense that no one really knows what the pain is like and what is like for a person/man/dad to handle, manage, and keep going.

I thought about this long and hard; what would I have wanted to hear from people 6 years ago and what would I want to hear every day that I remain alive that would help me? Many things that won't fit into one letter but I hope what I say goes some way to helping. It is not preaching, each journey is different, but it is said from the heart.

One thing though – you will be OK – remember this at the darkest times, remember this when it feels like you're going mad, when it feels like there's no hope, when you feel so angry.... Not that things will go back to how they were but just at some point the new 'normal' will be ok. This isn't just me saying it. Someone said it to me in the early days after Lily died and I didn't believe them and doubted it loads of times. They said that it will still be the same grief but just farther apart. This has proved true. But I am OK...more on this below.

I lost my precious daughter, Lily Isobel Kitterick, on the 16th June 2010. To say I could not have loved anything or anyone anymore is a complete understatement. Lily was mine and my wife's complete life. We lost her tragically and traumatically and we had our second child just 3 weeks later. This created and still does create chaos, regret, guilt, destruction, pain, anger, love, joy, etc., but we have 2 beautiful girls who have been my reason.

What I wanted to focus on is the anger. Why? Because I have struggled with this and still do. Anger at what happened, anger at myself for not stopping it, anger at why me, anger at people who care and then don't seem to care, anger at how life goes on, anger at how I have anger and don't know how to deal with it, anger at betrayal, anger at weakness, anger at lack of empathy, on and on and on....

I'm a man's man, physical and proud. I work in the education field and have counseled and taught thousands of children, worked with professionals and discussed anger and how we deal with it... let that, along with how grief works, go out the window when it comes to a father losing his child.

If my anger was a reaction to rational things maybe it could be dealt with in a rational way. But, referring to the above anger examples, it's not. Let me tell you what I have learnt about anger:

Your anger is justified and real, not time scaled or part of a process. You deal with it in the best way and safest way for you and your loved ones and DO NOT suppress it as we as males are seemingly programmed to do. It's OK to feel it. Feel it, do, you have to, it may scare you but you need to do it. Don't be too masculine, too proud, scared of it. Why would you not be angry?

I hope this has helped in the limited words I have. I will willingly talk to anyone who needs to talk with me and my contact is below. To finish; to love and to have what is so precious is to risk, joy and sorrow, it's the risk we take. I've learnt that too.

Andrew Kitterick

andrewkitterick@hotmail.com
twitter - @andrewkitterick
Father of Lily Isobel Kitterick

*"YOUR ANGER IS JUSTIFIED AND REAL,
NOT TIME SCALED OR PART OF A PROCESS.
YOU DEAL WITH IT IN THE BEST WAY AND
SAFEST WAY FOR YOU AND YOUR LOVED
ONES AND DO NOT SUPPRESS IT AS WE AS
MALES ARE SEEMINGLY PROGRAMMED
TO DO. IT'S OK TO FEEL IT. FEEL IT,
DO, YOU HAVE TO, IT MAY SCARE YOU
BUT YOU NEED TO DO IT. DON'T BE TOO
MASCULINE, TOO PROUD, SCARED OF IT.
WHY WOULD YOU NOT BE ANGRY?"*

DEAR FELLOW BEREAVED FATHER,

I first want to say I am extremely sorry for your loss. Nothing anyone can say will help with the pain that you are going through. All that anyone can do is help you navigate and listen to the hardship of this time in your life.

My wife and I loss our son at twenty-eight weeks. We found out that the chance of our son Johnathan surviving was slim when we went to our twenty-week ultrasound. We were told that he was a little smaller than what he should be, and that we should not be worried. However, we have made an appointment with Fetal Concerns at a different hospital.

When we walked into our appointment on Monday morning, we were told the worst news we could have ever been told. We were told that he had reverse flow in his cord. He was not getting everything he needed to survive.

When we were being told this, my wife was crying, and I had no idea what was happening. I felt so powerless, so not in control of my life anymore. All I wanted to do was vomit, and go back being naive to the world, and to the belief that nothing can happen after the first 12 weeks of pregnancy. We had appointment after appointment for the next 8 weeks until we could no longer see a heartbeat on the ultrasound.

The worst and best day of my life is when I got to see my son. He was perfect in every way. My wife and I were able to hold him for 30 hours. We tried to make as many memories as possible, within those 30 hours. We tried to fit 30 years of Christmas', birthdays, first day of schools, field trips, the first time he crawled, his first steps, first time he said Mom, and Dad, and the first time he said I love you. I revisit those 30 hours as often as I can.

As I am writing this, I am 18 months out from my loss. And in those eighteen months, many things have changed. I started a new job, we had our second child, and my outlook of life has changed. I am in a different place then I was eighteen months ago, but at a drop of a hat I can go back. I don't think that will ever go away, but you learn to live with it. Just like you learn to live with the invisible sign on your back saying that you lost a child.

If you would like to email me, I am more than happy to help you through your struggle as either a new bereaved father, or had a loss a long time ago. You are more than welcomed to email me at psmyth149@gmail.com

Paul

Father of Johnathan Paul Smyth

"THE WORST AND BEST DAY OF MY LIFE IS WHEN I GOT TO SEE MY SON. HE WAS PERFECT IN EVERY WAY. MY WIFE AND I WERE ABLE TO HOLD HIM FOR 30 HOURS. WE TRIED TO MAKE AS MANY MEMORIES AS POSSIBLE, WITHIN THOSE 30 HOURS. WE TRIED TO FIT 30 YEARS OF CHRISTMAS', BIRTHDAYS, FIRST DAY OF SCHOOLS, FIELD TRIPS, THE FIRST TIME HE CRAWLED, HIS FIRST STEPS, FIRST TIME HE SAID MOM, AND DAD, AND THE FIRST TIME HE SAID I LOVE YOU. I REVISIT THOSE 30 HOURS AS OFTEN AS I CAN."

DEAR GRIEVING FATHER,

I am so sorry for your loss, and for the pain and confusion you're probably feeling.

A few days after I found out our baby, Lucy, had died in her mother's womb, I spoke with a man who had suffered through multiple miscarriages. He told me something that I'd like to pass on to you: This sucks. It really sucks. And it hurts. And it's okay that it hurts. No one else gets to tell you how to suffer. If you're still hurting, even after the rest of the world says you should have recovered by now, it's okay to reach out for help. If you're starting to feel better, even though your wife is in a deep pit of grief, then be there for your wife. You might need to process your grief later, after she has started to recover.

At first, I mostly ignored my grief. When people asked how I was doing, I hid behind my wife's grief. "It's a lot harder for her, because she had bonded more with the baby." And that's probably true. But by saying that, I was taking all the attention away from myself. When people took my words at face value, and focused on how my wife was doing, I felt hurt and neglected.

Less than half a year after losing Lucy, we lost another baby, Elliot. I was angry. I had prayed so hard for God to let this baby live, and He didn't. I asked God, "Why did you put us through this again? Why didn't you let him live? You could have done something. Why didn't you?" I heard all kinds of answers from people, but none of them really satisfied me. And some answers, like "God needed another angel," just made me mad. First of all, God doesn't *need* anything. Secondly, rather than being comforting, this answer makes it sound like God deliberately acted and killed our baby so he could be in heaven.

The only answer that even came close was, "God only allows evil things to happen so that he can bring about a greater good." This one seemed the most honest. God didn't *cause* the evil, but he did *allow* it to happen. And a baby's death was not some good thing, it was in itself an evil. But God only allowed it so that he could bring about good. Well, that led to the question of what exactly this greater good was. I needed God to explain this plan to me, and then I would decide whether it was worth my child dying.

Then one day, something changed. I don't know if God spoke to me, or if I just had a realization myself. (I don't think the two are mutually exclusive.) But I suddenly had the thought, "I am not going to understand what God's plan is in all of this. I don't need to worry about that. I will trust that he has a plan, and hopefully one day it will make sense to me. It might not be until I am in heaven, reunited with Lucy and Elliot."

So if there's any advice that I can possibly offer you, it's that there aren't any perfect answers to the questions running through your mind. Or at least not any answers that will satisfy you right now. And that sucks. But that doesn't mean you can't ask the questions. Keep talking to your wife, and to your family and friends. Keep talking to God. Ask Him for understanding, and ask Him for peace. I will be praying for you, too.

My deepest condolences,

Matt Marks

Father of Lucy Anne Marks and Elliot Lourdes Marks
geekycatholicdad.blogspot.com

"THIS SUCKS. IT REALLY SUCKS. AND IT HURTS. AND IT'S OKAY THAT IT HURTS. NO ONE ELSE GETS TO TELL YOU HOW TO SUFFER. IF YOU'RE STILL HURTING, EVEN AFTER THE REST OF THE WORLD SAYS YOU SHOULD HAVE RECOVERED BY NOW, IT'S OKAY TO REACH OUT FOR HELP."

DEAR FATHERS,

In life we expect to witness the funerals of our grandparents and to bury our parents. That is simply the natural way of things, but we never expect to bury a child. We lost our son, Robert, in June 2009. Since then our life has been divided into two distinct periods - ‹before› and ‹after.› Nothing has ever been the same for us and sadly I expect this will be the same for you, your wife and family. You will all discover a 'new normal' where everything is slightly different as things will never be the same again. In photography terms, life lost its saturation, clarity and vibrancy. People say that time is a great healer, but time only blunts the stabbing knife of grief.

People will say the daftest things to you, many in the naive hope that their words will provide some solace. But we have found that folks simply don't know what to say and in the embarrassment and wanting to say something - they say something stupid. It's not their fault, they simply do not understand and hopefully will never have to understand what it is like to lose a child.

There is no hierarchy in the grief of a lost child. No matter how old they were, whether their death was sudden or expected, each death is completely unique. No one can really say "I know how you feel," as they can't know of the devastation and turmoil you and your family are feeling at the moment.

People who have lost a child can genuinely empathize and my wife and I found some help by joining a group of folk who have all lost a child. They are known as 'The Compassionate Friends' and our meetings and get-togethers allow us to openly talk about Robert - without the embarrassment or fear of others reactions.

I found the members of my camera club most supportive when I lost Robert. Some folk simply touched my arm and nodded - just to let me know that were thinking of me - but wisely not starting a conversion that would have led to tears. My wife didn't have that type of support and found that many of her friends simply avoided her. Men and women grieve differently. It is like a rollercoaster, sometimes you and your wife will be in the same cart but more often you'll be in different ones and while you're up she will be down. Yet society expects men to be strong, silent and 'keep a stiff upper lip.' This is, of course, complete nonsense.

A few months after Robert died I sought out some photos of when he was young and also happy times when he was older - and I made a slideshow. I often revisit this from time to time, whilst it almost always brings me to tears, it somehow raises my spirits afterwards.

It may still be the very early days, and I want to let you know that you are not alone.

Mark

Father of Robert

"THERE IS NO HIERARCHY IN THE GRIEF OF A LOST CHILD. NO MATTER HOW OLD THEY WERE, WHETHER THEIR DEATH WAS SUDDEN OR EXPECTED, EACH DEATH IS COMPLETELY UNIQUE. NO ONE CAN REALLY SAY "I KNOW HOW YOU FEEL," AS THEY CAN'T KNOW OF THE DEVASTATION AND TURMOIL YOU AND YOUR FAMILY ARE FEELING AT THE MOMENT."

TITLED: A FATHER'S PAIN: THE BIRTH THROUGH JIM'S EYES

I have heard some fathers express to me that they didn't feel particularly connected to their first child during the pregnancy, when the tiny person could only be experienced through light kicks, second hand recounting of movements from their wife, and blurry ultrasound photos where a head is only slightly distinguishable from a butt. It's only after they hold their newborn in their hands that lightning strikes and they feel that powerful, almost spiritual experience of becoming a father. It makes sense, but I am one of those weird ones who felt that feeling right from the beginning as soon as I learned my wife was pregnant.

I was overjoyed and felt far less anxiety over the prospect of raising a child than I would have thought I would. Every day I would place my head near my wife's belly and sing to my daughter, and I went to every appointment excited to see if we would learn something new. I learned, somewhat to my own surprise, that not only was I ready to be a father, it was what I wanted, really really wanted.

Unfortunately though, sometimes bad things happen.

After an otherwise remarkably smooth pregnancy, at 41 weeks my daughter passed. At this late stage my wife began to feel something was wrong and we went to the hospital 3 times over the course of about a week and each time were sent home because nothing was wrong (supposedly anyway). A day after the third dismissal my wife started bleeding heavily and, after we returned, we learned our baby had passed.

I remember the first time I felt what can only be described as a sensation similar to that of a knife being slowly pushed into my gut when moments before a problem was announced the two ultrasound techs working on my wife suddenly went from cheery and talkative to dead silent while casting nervous glances at each other, the image they were viewing having disquieted them.

That was the first arrival of the gut knife, but over the next few days it was my constant, unseen but hated companion that would twist itself painfully at each new stage of horror and grief.

I remember one of the things that got repeated over and over again in the pregnancy classes we went to was the following idea: "Pregnancy and child birth are hard, sometimes really hard, but it's all worth it when you are holding your child in your arms at the end."

Unfortunately we had to go through the labor process with

no hope of this reward and even worse, it was not a smooth process. What the doctors didn't know at the time was 1. my wife has a very narrow birth canal and 2. our baby was over nine pounds.

The birth lasted for hours, and despite both an epidural and additional pain killers my wife was in agony. During the process the doctors used forceps to try and remove my daughter but it did not go well, not well at all. At one point a doctor took me aside and, tears in her eyes started talking to me about a long string of what to my confused mind seemed unrelated facts: The forceps create great pressure when used in a situation like this. That my child had essentially been deceased a while and her body held in liquid which softens the flesh.

What are you trying to tell me? I eventually mumbled even as I realized the answer: That my child's body might come apart during this ordeal…..wonderful…another knife twist.

Eventually, after realizing they were making no progress, they offered me a choice of how to precede: One way or another, they would have to put my wife under because she was both in too much pain and was also losing strength. But they could either try to deliver vaginally in which case my child's body may be destroyed or they could do a cesarean but that had vastly increased health risks to my wife because of the circumstances. I told them to deliver vaginally if they could as I would rather have a healthy wife than a pretty child's body

They took her away and left me in the room, telling me they would inform me as things progressed. The place had been trashed by the high volume of traffic that had gone through it in the past few hours as doctors and nurses had worked to do what they could and there was what I considered at the time to be a frighteningly large amount of blood on the floor.

At this point I was extremely frightened for my wife's well-being and was afraid she would die and leave me alone, an irrational fear perhaps but events had already gone from normal life to scary horror movie in a shockingly short amount of time so it seemed not only possible, but likely in those moments. I sat for a long time on a couch in the room staring off into space.

I'm honestly not even sure how to explain how I felt at that time; fear, grief, rage and every other black emotion swirling like toxic sludge through my heart and brain, and of course my good friend the razor sharp blade worming its way deeper into my guts.

Eventually I stood and started pacing around the room mumbling to myself and crying softly. An hour passed and still no word, so I rang a nurse and demanded an update, and also that they clean the blood off the floor, and also some other things that I don't think made sense and I can't quite remember. She was very accommodating to my half mad ramblings and soon a doctor came to tell me that my wife was all right and the baby was delivered, they had done a pretty extreme episiotomy and it was just taking a while to stitch it up.

My relief was immense.

A woman came in and asked if I would like to see my baby in the meantime while waiting for my wife. I said yes. She warned me that it may be a bit gruesome but I said I still wanted to hold her. The brought her in a crib, fully dressed and with a little hat on her head. Her features were soft and beautiful and her body was warm but there was no mistaking her for a live baby. Her cheeks had fresh wounds in them and her body was limp, one arm had been badly broken and hung at an angle when I unwrapped the blanket she was in and inspected her body. I remember having the bizarre thought. "What I wanted was a beautiful baby girl. What I got was a beautiful baby girl who looks like she was savaged by wolves before they gave her to me."

At this point something broke inside me and I let out a long mournful wail that, even to my own ears, didn't sound like anything I'd ever heard a human throat make, this was followed by hysterical sobbing the likes of which not only had I never made before and I didn't even know I could make

Ah...at this point the memories are too painful for me to easily recount so I'm afraid I will have to skip ahead a bit.

A day and a half later my wife and I are in the recovery room resting and talking. We watch The Little Mermaid and my all time favorite movie, one I had wished to share with my daughter, Kung Fu Panda. Perhaps it is just the product of an over active imagination but I believe I feel my daughter in the room with us and I periodically tell her I love her.

My wife tells me she feels like a failure having lost our daughter and that she fears I will leave her in disgust. I tell her (to paraphrase a long conversation) to lock that shit in a box and dump it in the deepest trench of the ocean she can find. She is my one true love and I will never leave her. I will love her until long after the last of the stars in the sky have burnt out.

The recovery time to mourn my daughter is long and slow. My wife is prone to collapsing in tears at the slightest memory of my daughter and I deal with my grief by flying into rages about inconsequential annoyances, rarely addressing the true source of my pain as it is safer and more cathartic to tear apart straw targets than address a tragedy I cannot make right and can do nothing about.

I learn a different way of coping with my grief than what I classically do. Normally after a hard trauma I become sullen and withdrawn, I sleep a lot, shutting down like a computer that lags too much and needs to be rebooted for a fresh start. Here though I realize I cannot withdraw and must face my pain as straightforwardly as possible so that when my wife needs my emotional support I can be there for her.

The gut dagger is my constant companion, and sometimes it feels like I am bleeding out, hissing and spitting angrily as my life leaves me a drop at a time, But every day I tell my wife I love her and show her its true in every way I can. She is my rock and I need her.

Time passes, the wound doesn't heal, but it becomes less all consuming. I find joy in small things again, I look forward to having a rainbow baby. I will always miss my daughter and will likely think about her until the day I die.

I guess that's all I really have to say.

I love my sweet daughter Grace and my wonderful wife Sara is my whole world, top to bottom.

They are my girls, forever.

-Jim

Father of Grace Elizabeth Neau

*"THE RECOVERY TIME TO MOURN MY
DAUGHTER IS LONG AND SLOW. MY WIFE IS
PRONE TO COLLAPSING IN TEARS AT THE
SLIGHTEST MEMORY OF MY DAUGHTER
AND I DEAL WITH MY GRIEF BY FLYING
INTO RAGES ABOUT INCONSEQUENTIAL
ANNOYANCES, RARELY ADDRESSING
THE TRUE SOURCE OF MY PAIN AS IT IS
SAFER AND MORE CATHARTIC TO TEAR
APART STRAW TARGETS THAN ADDRESS A
TRAGEDY I CANNOT MAKE RIGHT AND CAN
DO NOTHING ABOUT."*

TO ALL OF THE FATHERS WHO ARE READING THIS LETTER:

I truthfully wish you weren't. I would not wish this kind of gut wrenching, mind bending, life altering pain on my worst enemy. My son Elliot was still born on May 19th, 2016. As I am writing this, it has only been 2 months since that day. I wish I could say all the empty colloquial things people say will help, but they won't. 'This will get easier,' 'This too shall pass,' 'Everything happens for a reason,' and so on will ignite so much anger or sadness within you that it will feel nearly impossible to focus after hearing it. Even someone saying 'Good Morning' to you day after day may become frustrating as it has to make you think whether or not it truthfully is a 'good' morning and, if you're early on in your grief, it probably doesn't feel like it is. This is all part of a new normal that you are finding within.

I'm not going to say any of these things I've mentioned above to you because I've realized how much they don't help. What I am going to tell you is that you have the right and permission to cry, the right and permission to be sad, and the right and permission to be angry. That said, I also wish the love that made you a father helps to carry you forward as you work with your grief day to day. (Note: I didn't say get through your grief, as this is something you will never get through nor get over.) I also said 'made you a father' because regardless of if you lost a child during a miscarriage, early term, full term, or a young child, we are all fathers. That is a powerful and important point to understand. You are a father, and nothing can take that away from you.

You're going to come to realize that there will be so many triggers early on that will cause you anger or sadness of varying degrees. It could be as deep as celebrating a birthday of yours or your partner after your loss, or as inane as a freshly painted or newly noticed 'Expecting Mothers' parking space. The pain from these triggers will range from uncontrollable crying or anger, to feeling like you've been hit with an invisible bullet in your heart that makes you wince away. If I've learned anything over these 2 long months I would say that is it's important to share these triggers or experiences with your partner, your loved ones, or whomever will listen. Sharing of any kind means you're acknowledging your pain and that helps work with grief as the waves of it come and go.

As some other books such as Grieving Dads will point out, you're also potentially trying to be supportive or be strong for your wife or your partner. This however does not mean to avoid sharing your feelings with them. Knowing how flat out gutted you are, and that you're just as upset as they are, is just as important as helping or caring for them when they're feeling the same. I may not be visibly upset on the same level or the same frequency as my wife, but when I'm hurting I am not afraid to collapse in a crying embrace with her. This is not a sign of weakness, far from it. This shows exactly how much pain I'm in, and that I'm just as hurt over our loss even though I may not show it externally in the same way, or with the same frequency.

I hope this letter can help at least one person with a similar story to mine. Please know you are not alone. Sadly, there are many more of us than anyone likes to admit or talk about. I'm sorry you're are now a part of this community, I wish you didn't have to be.

Jamie

Father of Elliot

"WHAT I AM GOING TO TELL YOU IS THAT YOU HAVE THE RIGHT AND PERMISSION TO CRY, THE RIGHT AND PERMISSION TO BE SAD, AND THE RIGHT AND PERMISSION TO BE ANGRY. THAT SAID, I ALSO WISH THE LOVE THAT MADE YOU A FATHER HELPS TO CARRY YOU FORWARD AS YOU WORK WITH YOUR GRIEF DAY TO DAY. (NOTE: I DIDN'T SAY GET THROUGH YOUR GRIEF, AS THIS IS SOMETHING YOU WILL NEVER GET THROUGH NOR GET OVER.) I ALSO SAID 'MADE YOU A FATHER' BECAUSE REGARDLESS OF IF YOU LOST A CHILD DURING A MISCARRIAGE, EARLY TERM, FULL TERM, OR A YOUNG CHILD, WE ARE ALL FATHERS. THAT IS A POWERFUL AND IMPORTANT POINT TO UNDERSTAND. YOU ARE A FATHER, AND NOTHING CAN TAKE THAT AWAY FROM YOU."

DEAR FATHERS,

Where do I start? Our little boy Brodie was born on 28 march 2013 and died 3 days later. I won't go into all the detail, just to say it was a text book pregnancy but something went wrong at delivery and the damage Brodie sustained couldn't be recovered from. There were no issues with the hospital just very very unlucky (Brodie's was the 2nd case at that time out of circa 30,000 deliveries in the consultant's 5 years at that hospital). In some ways it doesn't make it easier, but at least there is not anger directed towards someone. I would hate for that to be the case.

In some ways I was the lucky one. I got to see Brodie with his eyes open, crying and holding my thumb. That was the moment for me. Changed my life right there and then. I was nervous about being a dad, but Brodie made me realise that I shouldn't be. All I wanted to do was protect and save, him but I couldn't do either sadly. His mummy didn't get to hold him when he was awake and I know this is so difficult for her. We did get to hold him for 3 hours before he passed which was so precious to us

What can I say which might help? I'm not sure. Every case is different so don't compare - others will do that for you. Whilst it is very touching that others try to empathize with you, it might be the case that their experience doesn't mirror that of your own. Remember if you can that sometimes people reaching out in such a way might also be therapy for them as much as for you as their lives also changed forever at that time.

There is no right and wrong way to deal with it. The only must is to be there for your other half. Her heart will be broken and she is likely to be a different person forever. Just be there - it may involve conversation, it may not. Just be close by if at all possible.

Acceptance - probably the most relevant word. People say move on etc., but it isn't the right word for me. I think about Brodie first thing in the morning and last at night and often during the day as you can't escape family conversations at work or stop wondering what might have been. Your mind and body get used to the pain and you learn to deal with it better as you accept how you feel and don't fight it. There will be good and bad moments and that is just a sad reality.

Anger, blame and what ifs will be there. Accept this and take time to process and let them pass. They are emotions, understandable, but I am afraid there are no answers, just the fact of where you are and that you have to get through this day the best you can. Take each day as a battle, win small victories, and as time passes you will learn to deal with it.

Anniversaries are especially tough, but I say just do what you would have done - get a cake, be together and go spend time with the little one. We go every Sunday to see Brodie. It was going to be our family day anyway - why should that change even though he isn't here?

Go and speak to a professional when you both feel able. The hospital should be able to help. It was probably the best thing we did. Our psychologist was amazing and really helped guide us through our feelings and emotions. We still read his letter now. Also groups like Sands, for example, can be of great comfort. However, don't feel like you have to bond with one person, be willing to meet with several to see if you connect. Support is there for you if you want to seek it out. It's often easier for strangers to help than friends or family if they aren't the type of people who can chat about such events

When such sad events take place they don't make sense and they challenge your values/beliefs. They will put great strain on your relationships with friends, family and work. The most important thing, in my opinion, is your partner - do whatever it takes to be the rock she needs. You will also need help and be ready to ask as she will for sure at some point ask how you are doing. From such a tragedy the result could be the end of a relationship or it can make you stronger as a couple. This is the one thing you can control - what you want the outcome to be and work towards it. Manage to cope with this and you will be a more aware, caring and compassionate couple.

We went on to have our second child - Maggie. She is now just about to be 2. Whilst being amazing and the light of my/ our life she doesn't "fix" what happened to Brodie. However your brain can only deal with so much and she is a focus for us. As events unfold we are still continually reminded of what we missed with Brodie - this really hurts and reminds us that he is always a part of the family. Just because he isn't around doesn't change this.

Life will feel like it stops after such a loss. However, for others the world keeps spinning and you will notice this. With time you will see things progressing - maybe through going back to work or other events happening (some sad and happy) which take your focus for a while. You will always come back to the loss, but try to take time and roll with the punches the best you can, be there for your partner, and communicate as much as you can.

I hope this helps.

Greg Munro

Father of Brodie Munro

"ACCEPTANCE - PROBABLY THE MOST RELEVANT WORD. PEOPLE SAY MOVE ON ETC., BUT IT ISN'T THE RIGHT WORD FOR ME. I THINK ABOUT BRODIE FIRST THING IN THE MORNING AND LAST AT NIGHT AND OFTEN DURING THE DAY AS YOU CAN'T ESCAPE FAMILY CONVERSATIONS AT WORK OR STOP WONDERING WHAT MIGHT HAVE BEEN. YOUR MIND AND BODY GET USED TO THE PAIN AND YOU LEARN TO DEAL WITH IT BETTER AS YOU ACCEPT HOW YOU FEEL AND DON'T FIGHT IT. THERE WILL BE GOOD AND BAD MOMENTS AND THAT IS JUST A SAD REALITY."

Dear Grieving Dad,

I wish someone had told me this when I was fresh in the grief from the death of my son:

You are not alone.

Most men are taught to keep grief inside. Most of us don't talk about things like this with our friends. Grief is something we're supposed to deal with in silence. Sometimes we aren't even allowed to have a bad day. Once, a few weeks after my son died, I was driving to work. The sun was rising and the sky was a beautiful cotton-candy pink. For no particular reason, I thought of my son, who died at not quite 22 weeks gestation. With a heavy heart I went to work.

Walking in, I saw someone who I knew only in passing. "How are you?"

"Not having a great day today," I said. "I'm feeling sad about my son."

That person reported me to management as "being a threat to myself and others".

The misunderstanding was quickly cleared up, but it left me with a lasting sense that I shouldn't discuss my grief with anyone.

But things don't have to be this way. Please don't be like I was and keep these feelings trapped inside yourself. There are other dads out there who have lost children. Many of our letters are collected here. Reach out to us. No one can understand your particular grief except you, but we do understand what it's like to grieve and deal with loss.

Please reach out and find someone to talk with. That includes me. Here is my email: darrellfpaul@gmail.com. I have no magic answers for grief. No one does. But maybe I can help you feel a little better, or at least, a little listened-to.

With great sympathy,

Darrell Paul.

a fellow grieving Dad
Father of William Edward Paul and Noah Matthew Paul

*"I WISH SOMEONE HAD TOLD ME THIS
WHEN I WAS FRESH IN THE GRIEF FROM
THE DEATH OF MY SON:*

YOU ARE NOT ALONE."

DEAR FATHERS,

Where do I begin.

Well, I remember the exact moment that we were told that our baby didn't have a heartbeat. "I'm so sorry" was all that we were told, those few words destroyed our entire universe - our little girl was gone. We were then part of a club that no parent should be, we had to bury a much loved child before her life had begun. We had hopes and dreams of what our daughter's life would have been.

To start with I was scared to talk about what had happened, not because I didn't want to talk about her, but because I was aware of making other people feel uncomfortable. You can see it in their faces, the not knowing what to say. When in reality there is nothing that can be said, apart from "I'm sorry." It wasn't till I plucked up the courage to tell people that I have three children, that I realized just how many other people have had the same experience as me. Little one's with little wings that never leave your heart or thoughts.

It has taken me many years to not be scared to talk about her, our little "Seren." Now I'll tell anybody who asks, I want everybody to know that my little girl did exist. In a strange way it makes me feel better. Stay strong, I don't think that it gets any easier, you just learn how to exist and then live with the pain. Shout their names from the tallest mountains for all to hear and, most importantly, remember that there will always be somebody there to help, just reach out.

Take care of you and your loved ones.

Andrew

Father to Severn Evelyn Jones

"IT HAS TAKEN ME MANY YEARS TO NOT BE SCARED TO TALK ABOUT HER, OUR LITTLE "SEREN." NOW I'LL TELL ANYBODY WHO ASKS, I WANT EVERYBODY TO KNOW THAT MY LITTLE GIRL DID EXIST. IN A STRANGE WAY IT MAKES ME FEEL BETTER."

FROM FATHER TO FATHER

"Take deep breaths and let the pain wash over you like a wave."

That's what my wife's doctor told her as she was laboring to deliver our twin boys, Drazan and Damon, nearly 16 weeks shy of full term. Our boys did not survive, and that day in the hospital was filled with all the emotions you've no doubt experienced with the loss of your child.

Over the following weeks and months, as those emotions resurfaced, I would remind myself of those words. "Take deep breaths and let the pain wash over you like a wave." Because sometimes the grief would grab a hold of me and squeeze so tightly that I didn't know which way to turn. And it's during times like those that I needed to slow down – way down – in order to come out the other side.

Looking back on those days from a distance of two-and-a-half years, I can see that there were little things that brought me comfort. When we arrived home from the hospital, my wife fell asleep on the couch and I started washing the dishes. Having a simple task to complete was soothing, and in the days that followed I made a conscious effort to engage in the activities of daily life: making meals, cleaning the litter box, washing the dishes.

These are small things, but completing them gave me a sense of accomplishment while everything else was falling apart.

If you have other children, then caring for them (and for yourself) will keep you grounded through the difficult first few weeks. If not, then it may seem like everything in your life has come to a standstill. My wife and I did not have other children at the time, and we had been preparing furiously for our boys to arrive. And then, all of sudden, they were gone and so was all of the urgency and anxiousness we felt during my wife's pregnancy. It was a sad, empty feeling.

In the immediate aftermath of our loss, I was able to take some time off work, and I recommend you do the same if possible. As lonely as those days can be, they are also a time to mourn and to collect yourself, and to reckon with the shock of what has happened.

During my time off work, I made sure to leave the house once a day for an errand or a drive or…something. I called and texted with friends and family members who had been there to share the exciting news. I also found moments of comfort: riding my bike to the beach on a warm weekday, watching the San Antonio Spurs steamroll the Miami Heat in the NBA Finals, repairing a foosball table that my wife and I found at a thrift store. You will probably find solace and sadness alike in the most commonplace of moments.

After I went back to work, and as the weeks and months passed, I found myself turning to writing to sort through my feelings. I would journal from time to time about everything from my sons to my marriage to my job, and all of the other things that occupied space in my head. I also found it helpful to exercise, and developed a daily elliptical machine habit to help alleviate stress.

But one of the most helpful things for me – a Godsend, really – was talking to other couples who had been through the same thing. You may notice, when you break the news to people, that more of them than you ever expected have suffered a similar loss. This isn't something that people tend to talk about, but you will find that you are far from alone. If a friend, or relative, or co-worker offers you the opportunity to talk, take them up on it.

I'd also recommend seeking out a support group for parents who've suffered pregnancy or infant loss. My wife and I found just such a group through our hospital, and it was very helpful to meet other people who were going through the same thing. We gathered once a month in a lovely room in one of the administrative buildings, and those meetings meant the world to us.

You may also be wondering what to do in terms of a funeral or memorial. For some people, it is obvious that they want a funeral. My wife's cousin lost a child several years before we did, and he planned a funeral for his son. But it's not a requirement. We had our sons cremated, and a friend of ours made custom boxes for their heart-shaped urns that we keep displayed on our mantle. It's a lovely tribute, and one that made sense for us. In time, you'll find a way to memorialize your child as well.

And that's the final thing...time. Whatever brings you comfort, or keeps you grounded, or helps you understand your feelings in the wake of your loss will also help you move through the days to a time when it doesn't hurt quite so much. It might sound impossible at this moment, but that time will arrive. In the meantime, be kind to yourself, connect with other parents who have felt the same thing, and remember your child in whatever way makes sense for you.

And if all else fails, just take deep breaths and let the pain wash over you like a wave.

Dixon Galvez-Searle

Father of Drazan and Damon

*"TAKE DEEP BREATHS AND LET THE PAIN
WASH OVER YOU LIKE A WAVE."*

DEAR DADS,

Well this sucks, doesn't it? It doesn't get much worse than this, it's true. It's still a journey you're on now, but it's a very different one, not one that either of us wanted. But you will survive. When we lost Henry, stillborn on 2nd May 2014, I had so many different emotions going around in my head. This may sound familiar to you.

Grief, of course, the most overwhelming grief that exists... grief the like of which I didn't even know was possible... Pride - I'm a dad now, after all. That's my little boy in those photos. He's real, he exists. Nothing and no-one can ever take that away from me... My survival instinct kicked in - just got to get my head down and get through this, right? There's good news and bad news on this front. You don't ever really "get over" this I don't think, you just find a course to navigate that allows you to cope. My overriding sense was an instinct to put my own emotions to one side and focus on protecting my wife, Briony. So for weeks and months afterwards, I plastered on a smile and handled the question "how's she doing?", whilst all the time resisting the overwhelming urge to shout "WHAT ABOUT ME? HE'S MY SON TOO!"

Did I break down? Yes - but only in private, or with a tiny handful of people that I trusted with the absolute inner sanctum of my emotions. Got to keep the front up, not show any weakness or fallibility. We're men after all, we have to stay strong, right? WRONG. This is your son or your daughter too. You'll want to put that front up sometimes, and that's fine. But don't deny yourself your own grieving process. I managed it for about ten months, and then came crashing down. Find some release, some outlet for your grief. It might be just one friend that has experienced the horror of losing a child, it might be someone who you didn't think of as a really close friend, but really steps up to the plate.

If your journey is anything like ours, you'll have a really honest re-evaluation of your friendship circle about three to six months after the loss of your precious child. Some of those that you thought were your closest friends will have gone AWOL, completely gone off the grid. Some of those that were barely passing acquaintances - more evening guests at your wedding, but not close enough to get an invite to the ceremony - they'll have really gone flying up the league table. You may also have found a support group or network of parents that have been through a similar loss. Everyone thinks those are for the mums though, don't they? A load of women sitting around crying about their dead babies. We joined a support group in our town, Our Angels - I wanted to go, Briony didn't - and discovered that wasn't the case AT ALL. The women (and men) in that group are now, without a doubt, our closest group of friends in the world. Don't be afraid or unwilling to reach out - the truth is, your existing friends won't have the faintest clue how to support you through this. Some will do a better job of it than others, but unless they've been there themselves, they just won't get it.

So here's my message. It's not a one-size fits all solution (there's no perfect solution), but here goes. You won't ever get over the loss of your precious child. But you will get through it. Life does return to normal, it's just a "new normal" now. Don't be too hard on yourself. Keep talking to people. If people can't handle you talking about your emotions and about your child, you don't need them in your life any more.

One more thing. You're allowed to mention your child's name. Talk about your son or daughter if you want. You're a dad, you can talk about them all you want. Your true friends now will not only understand that, they'll talk about your child too. They'll always remember them too.

Reach out. Ask for help. Accept help.

But remember, you don't have to take the weight of the world on your shoulders. You're a dad now too...and you're not alone. Stay strong,

Chris

Father of Henry Oliver Mills-Binnie

www.ourangelscharity.co.uk

"BUT REMEMBER, YOU DON'T HAVE TO TAKE THE WEIGHT OF THE WORLD ON YOUR SHOULDERS. YOU'RE A DAD NOW TOO...AND YOU'RE NOT ALONE."

OH YOU BRAVE, BRAVE FATHER,

From the bottom of my heart, I want you to know that you are not alone. While there are so few people in the world who can truly understand your devastation, I do. We do, and we are here for you. In the days, weeks, months, and years to come, you may hear some say, "Don't worry. You'll have another baby." I know they don't understand. They can't. For them, it is impossible to comprehend the crippling scope of all that you've lost.

You lost the comfort of coming home to your cooing baby and her glowing mother. You lost the weight of her in your arms. You lost the joy of watching his first steps and the thrill of his first words. You lost lullabies and bedtime stories. You lost play dates and playgrounds. You lost temper tantrums, tender moments, and sweet little toes. You lost first days of school and summer vacations. You lost tee ball games and field trips and parent-teacher conferences. You lost first dates, birthdays, holidays, and graduations. You lost their incredible talent, their fiery spirit, their brilliant mind, their sensitive heart. You lost your hopes and dreams for who your precious baby could become. You lost your role as teacher, caretaker, provider, and protector. You lost a part of yourself. You lost your future.

In March of 2016, we lost our sweet daughter, Mathilda, shortly before her birth at 40 weeks and 4 days. For me, every day remains a labyrinth of worry and wonder and where to go next. These are endless empty days, all full of quiet and stillness where there should be a cacophony and constant motion. I am perpetually engulfed by the burning awareness of how different my life should be. To think that I could have anything of value to offer you feels arrogant and heavy. However, there are some things I've been told that I think you should know.

You are a father. More than that, you are the strongest and most courageous kind of father. You love and nurture a baby you can never hold.

You did nothing wrong. This is not your fault. There is nothing you could have done to save your child.

Your grief is normal. If you have a hat your baby wore and you want to kiss it goodnight, do it. If you want to stare in the sky and tell them about your day, go for it. Read them stories. Preserve their nursery. Plant flowers and build a birdhouse for them. Honor them in any way that fills your soul. Nobody can tell you how to parent your dead child. Nobody can judge your grief.

Be patient with yourself and your baby's mother. There is no timetable for grief. There is no getting over so devastating a loss. All you can do is learn to live with it. Like any weight, it may get lighter the longer you lift it, but it will always be yours to carry.

My darling Mathilda was arrestingly beautiful, just like her mother. She had her mom's hands, but she had my skin. She had my hair, but she had her mom's nose. She was our sweet Peanut, our first daughter and our only child. The days and months since we lost her have been the darkest of my life. The only light that I've found has been in the belief that she is the energy that drives all of the wonder in the world. She is the sun that warms my skin and she's the snow in my hair. She's the waves that crash, the breeze that cools, and the rains that bring life. She's the leaves that fall and she's the sand between my toes. She is every bird song, every butterfly, and every rainbow. She fills my world with all of the beauty she can muster, and I find her in that. I find her everywhere I can.

You are an intrepid father, loyal and true. In time, I hope that you can find some of what you lost.

In hope and solidarity,

Jonathan.

Mathilda's Daddy

Born Still on March 4th, 2016
www.lostlullabies.weebly.com

"YOU ARE A FATHER.

YOU DID NOTHING WRONG.

YOUR GRIEF IS NORMAL.

BE PATIENT WITH YOURSELF AND YOUR BABY'S MOTHER.

YOU ARE AN INTREPID FATHER, LOYAL AND TRUE."

ONLINE RESOURCES FOR SUPPORT

www.emilyrlong.com

https://www.facebook.com/groups/inkandpaperhealing/

www.AFatherOfLoss.com

Essay "To Grieve": http://www.performancephilosophy.org/journal/article/view/10/27

https://www.facebook.com/mjsmemories/

www.stillstandingmag.com

https://www.facebook.com/GrievingDads/

https://www.facebook.com/groups/Grievingfathers/

http://maya.stephenson.muchloved.com

geekycatholicdad.blogspot.com

"Too Wonderful (Asher's Song)" https://www.youtube.com/watch?v=xnLcTc0rUzg

http://www.facebook.com/mannysfund

www.lostlullabies.weebly.com

www.ourangelscharity.co.uk

OTHER AVAILABLE BOOKS BY EMILY:

Invisible Mothers: When Love Doesn't Die (September 2015)

You Are Not Alone: Love Letters from Loss Mom to Loss Mom (April 2016)

UPCOMING BOOKS:

Life Without the Baby Journal: Redefining Life,

Motherhood and Self After Loss (pending March 2017)

Made in the USA
Las Vegas, NV
13 July 2021

26323088R00075